Home Learning Series
Activities
Level A

Calico Spanish Home Learning Series
Activities Level A

Second Edition

Author: Sara-Elizabeth Cottrell
Contributing Editor: Erica Fischer

Copyright © 2015 Kids Immersion, LLC. All rights reserved.

No part of this publication may be reproduced, stored in a retrieval system, or transmitted in any form or by any means, electronic, mechanical, photocopy, recording, or any other — except for brief quotations embodied in critical articles or printed reviews — without prior written permission of the publisher.

Published by:
Kids Immersion, LLC
PO Box 498
Mt. Hood, OR 97041
USA
Ph: 888-375-8484
Fx: 888-375-0606
E-mail: support@calicospanish.com

Printed in the United States of America.

August 2015

Table of Contents

Lección 1: Es azul 4

Lección 1: ¡Hola y adiós! 5

Lección 1: ¿Cómo te llamas, animal? 6

Lección 2: ¿Cuántos hay? 7

Lección 2: ¡Es grande! 8

Lección 2: ¿Cuántos años tienes? 9

Lección 3: Diciembre en la familia de María .. 10

Lección 3: Día de la semana 12

Lección 4: Es amarillo 13

Lección 4: ¿Cómo estás? 14

Lección 4: ¿Bien o mal? 15

Lección 5: ¡Es pequeño! 16

Lección 5: ¿Quién dice … ? 17

Lección 5: Así soy 18

Lección 6: ¿Te gusta? 20

Lección 6: ¡Me gusta! 21

Lección 7: Tengo, no tengo 22

Lección 7: ¿Cantar o saltar? 23

Lección 7: ¡Soy especial! 24

Lección 8: Puedo, no puedo 25

Lección 8: Sí, ¡se puede! 26

Song Lyrics 27

    ¿Cómo te llamas?
    (What's your name?) 27

    Hola a todos
    (Hello everyone) 28

    Lluvia
    (Rain) 29

    ¿Cuántos años tienes?
    (How old are you?) 30

    La semana
    (The week) 31

    Elefantes grande
    (Big elephants) 32

    Colores, colores
    (Colors, colors) 33

    Vengan ya
    (Come right now) 34

    Caballito blanco
    (Little white horse) 35

    Chocolate
    (Chocolate) 36

El calendario 37

Mapa de América del Sur 38

*Mapa de México, América Central
y el Caribe* 39

Mapa de España 39

Suggested Answers 40

Lección 1

Es azul

Draw four items in your home that are *azul*. Color them.

Can you show your drawings to someone and describe each thing by saying *es azul*? Write below each drawing: *Es azul.*

1.

2.

3.

4.

Lección 1

¡Hola y adiós!

What would they say? In the speech bubble, write what you think each person might say in the situation shown. Your choices are in the word bank.

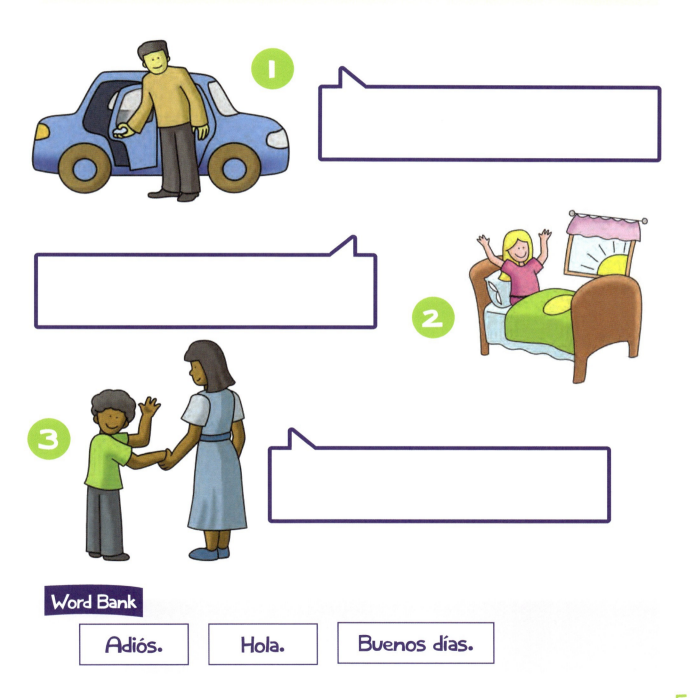

Word Bank

Adiós.   Hola.   Buenos días.

Lección 1: ¿Cómo te llamas, animal?

How does the *pez* tell you his name? He says, "*Me llamo Pedro.*"

Write *Me llamo* and each animal's name in the corresponding speech bubble to show how he or she would answer the question *¿Cómo te llamas?*

Extension

When you are finished, color the animals blue and try to describe the color. Can you say "*es azul*" to describe each animal?

Notes: Direct the question *¿Cómo te llamas?* to each animal. Have the children respond as if they are the animal. In English, this would be: What is your name? My name is …. In Spanish, the format is: *¿Cómo te llamas? Me llamo ….* First answer orally, then fill in the box next to each animal. Suggested answers are on page 40.

Lección 2

¿Cuántos hay?

Pepe wants to know, "*¿Cuántos hay?*"

Count the objects in Spanish and use the word bank to help you write out the word for the number.

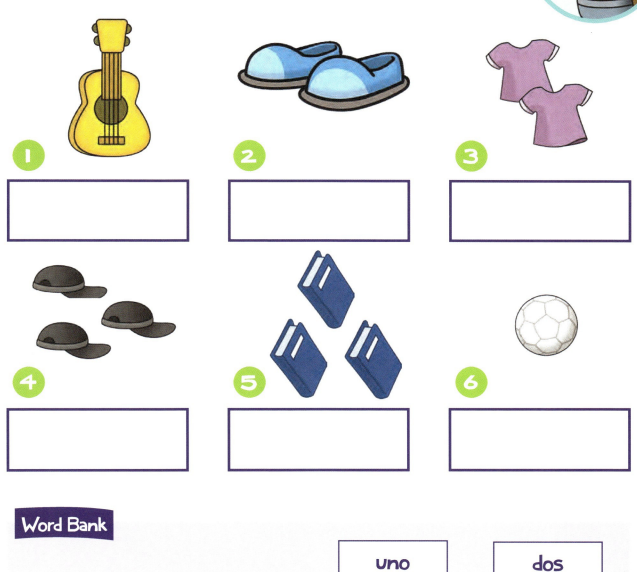

Word Bank

uno   dos

tres   uno   dos   tres

Lección 2

¡Es grande!

Look at the pictures. In each pair of objects, one item *es grande*. Circle the one that is *grande*. Show your sheet to someone and describe each large item by saying, *"Es grande."*

Lección 2

¿Cuántos años tienes?

Carlos is asking our animal friends "*¿Cuántos años tienes?*"

Can you help the animals tell him how old they are? See how high you can count in Spanish by counting the candles on the cakes. In each speech bubble, write the appropriate description: *Tengo (#) años.*

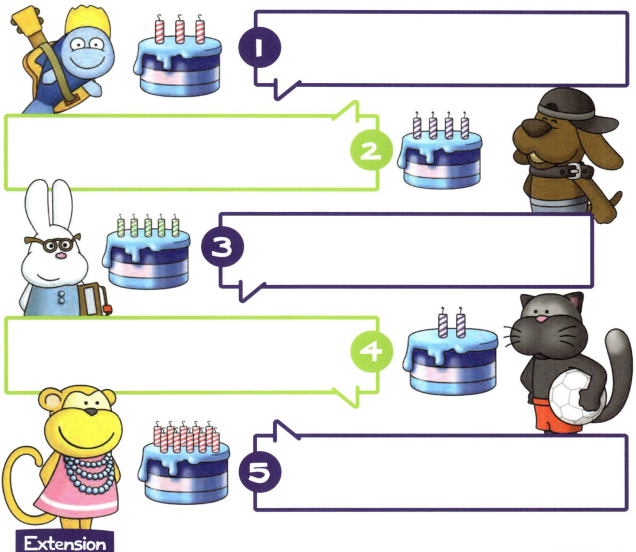

Extension

Circle in *azul* each animal that can say, "*¡Soy muy grande!*"

Notes: Children are taught to count to three in Level A. If you wish, you may use this worksheet to introduce counting to ten in Spanish by referencing the numbers poster. Alternatively, count the number of candles beyond three using English.

If your child is not ready for writing independently, simply practice the questions and answers orally and then fill in the blanks for the child with the correct sentences.
Have children hold up the correct number of fingers for each animal's age before you fill in the blanks.

Diciembre en la familia de María

It's December and María's family has a lot going on!
On what day are these special things happening for her family this month? Beside the pictures on the next page, write the Spanish word for the day of that event.

lunes	martes	miércoles	jueves	viernes	sábado	domingo
	1	2	3	4	5 🏀	6
7	8	9 🎂	10	11	12	13
14	15	16	17	18	19	20 🦒ZOO
21	22 🧳	23	24	25 🎄	26	27
28	29	30	31 🎈			

10

Lección 3: Día de la semana

Pedro wants to know, "¿Qué día es?"

Help his animal *amigos* answer that question by writing *es* and the day shown with a star on that animal's week chart. Then, pretend that you are the animal shown. Someone can ask you, "¿Qué día es?" and you should tell him or her what day it is. After that, switch roles and you ask, "¿Qué día es?"

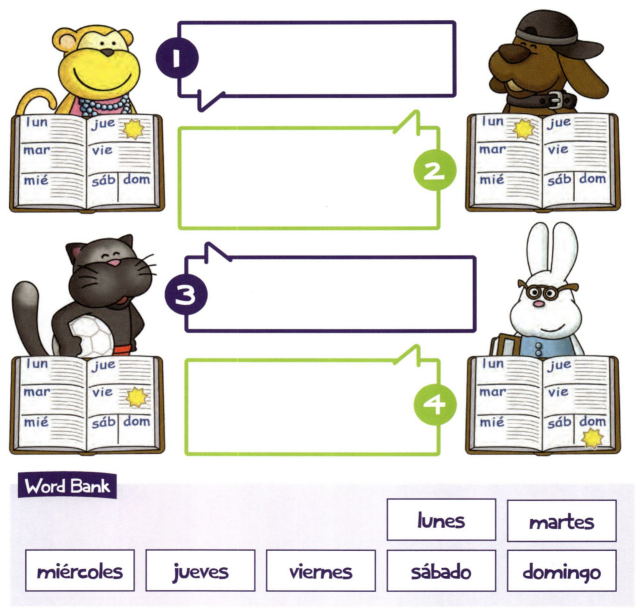

Word Bank

| lunes | martes | miércoles | jueves | viernes | sábado | domingo |

Notes: Fill in the blanks using the word bank to help with the spelling of each day of the week. Alternatively, you can cut out the words and help children match them to each blank then write *Es* followed by the word (day of the week.) Remember, the days of the week are not capitalized in Spanish except when they are the first word in a sentence. If your child is not ready for writing independently, simply practice the questions and answers orally and then fill in the blanks for the child with the correct sentences.

Lección 4

Es amarillo

Draw four items in your home that are *amarillo*. Color them.

Show your drawings to someone and describe each thing by saying "*Es amarillo.*" Write below each drawing: *Es amarillo*.

1.

2.

3.

4.

Lección 4
¿Cómo estás?

Pedro wants to know how his friends are doing.

He is asking them, "*¿Cómo estás?*" Write in the speech bubbles how each friend answers the question — either *estoy bien* or *estoy mal*.

Extension

Color each animal either *azul* or *amarillo*. Then go back and identify the color of each animal by saying either, "*Es azul,*" or "*Es amarillo.*"

Notes: Children can complete this worksheet and then color the animals. If you use blue and yellow to color the animals, then you can ask children to describe the animals by saying, "*Es azul,*" or "*Es amarillo.*"

If your child is not ready for independent writing, complete the worksheet orally, and fill in the answers for them. You can also ask the children to draw a happy face or sad face next to each picture and then restate the proper responses: "*Estoy mal.*" "*Estoy bien.*"

Lección 4

¿Bien o mal?

Survey five people or stuffed animals and find out how they're doing.

In the first column, write the person or animal's name. Then, ask them, "*¿Cómo estás?*" and check the answer they give: *bien* or *mal*. The first one is an example.

Name	Bien	Mal
Julian	x	

Notes: If you have a big enough group, children can survey one another. If you do not have enough people to survey five individuals, simply have your child survey stuffed animals or pets. You can give a reply for how the animal is feeling.

If your child is not ready for independent writing, complete the worksheet orally, and fill in the answers for them. You can also ask the children to draw a happy face or sad face to illustrate the answer and then restate the proper responses: *mal* or *bien*.

¡Es pequeño!

Look at the pictures. One item in each pair of objects *es pequeño*. Circle the one that is *pequeño*. Show your sheet to a friend and describe it by saying, "*Es pequeño.*"

Lección 5: ¿Quién dice ... ?

Look at the pictures.
From the word bank, write the phrase that the character could use to describe itself.

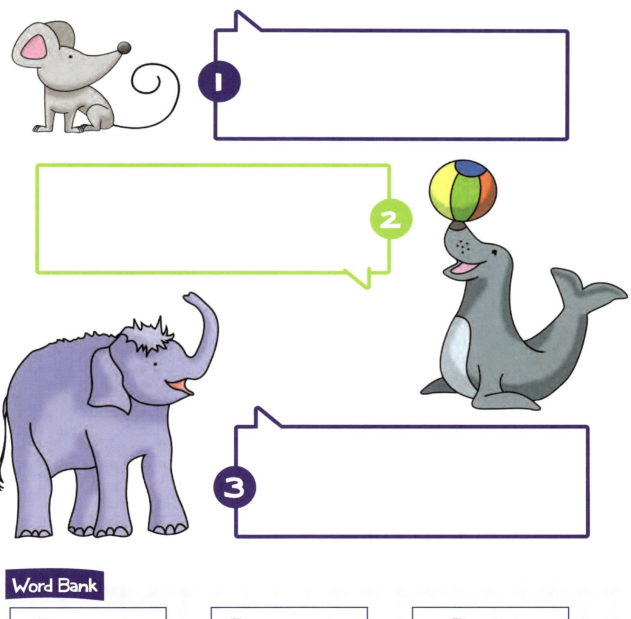

Word Bank

| Soy grande. | Soy pequeño. | Soy lista. |

Lección 5

Así soy

Can you describe yourself?

Draw a picture of yourself in the frame on the next page. Be sure to color some items blue or yellow (*azul* or *amarillo*). Then write two sentences that start with the word *soy* to describe yourself. Examples: *Soy listo, soy grande, soy pequeño*. (Remember, adjectives — describing words — that end in "o" will change to "a" for girls: *listo* to *lista* and *pequeño* to *pequeña*.)

1 ....

2 ....

3 ....

4 ....

5 ....

Extension

On lines 3, 4, and 5, can you also write how you would tell someone your name, how old you are, and how you are doing?

Notes: The directions encourage children to use blue and yellow when drawing the picture. Use this opportunity to continue repeating the color words *azul* and *amarillo*. For example: Are you going to use *azul* or *amarillo* for your shirt? For your hair?

Answers will vary, but some suggestions are given on page 40. If your child is not ready for independent writing, complete the worksheet orally, and fill in the answers for them.

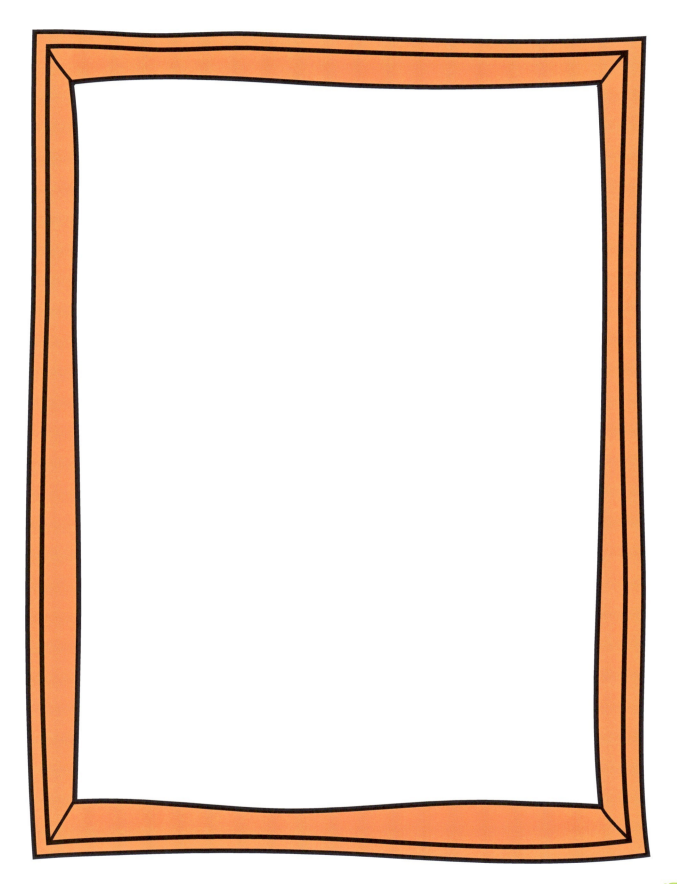

¿Te gusta?

Above each word, draw a picture that illustrates that word. For the color words, draw an item that is *azul* or *amarillo*. Then, circle your opinion about the item you drew: *me gusta* or *no me gusta*.

azul

 me gusta   no me gusta

amarillo

 me gusta   no me gusta

saltar

 me gusta   no me gusta

cantar

 me gusta   no me gusta

Lección 6

¡Me gusta!

María la mona wants to know which foods you like.

María asks, "*¿Te gusta?*"

Label each item with *me gusta* or *no me gusta*.

....

   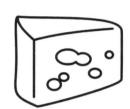   

....

....

Extension

Can you show which items are usually *amarillo*? Color those foods *amarillo*.
After coloring each item, describe them by saying, "*Es amarillo.*"

Notes: Each child will answer this worksheet differently depending on his or her food preference. Simply ask your child, "*¿Te gusta?*"
The English and Spanish names of each item are listed here for your reference. However, it is not necessary to use the Spanish names of the food items in completing this worksheet.
la cebolla (the onion), *la piña* (the pineapple),
la sopa (the soup), *el queso* (the cheese),
la hamburguesa (the hamburger),
la banana (the banana), *el jugo de naranja* (the orange juice)

Lección 7
Tengo, no tengo

Do you have these things that María and Pedro have?

Below each picture, circle *tengo* or *no tengo*. Then show your sheet to someone and tell them what you have (*tengo*) or do not have (*no tengo*).

Extension

Can you use the words for these objects? They are in the stories but have not been in your vocabulary. Try to use *tengo* and *no tengo* with these words: *pelo, guitarra, collares, tenis*. Next to each item, write the Spanish word for its color.

Lección 7

¿Cantar o saltar?

Next to each character, write which activity they like to do: *cantar* or *saltar*.

1 ....

3 ....

2 ....

4 ....

5 ....

¡Soy especial!

Lección 7

Using the word bank (words can be used more than once), fill in the statements about María and Pedro. When you are finished, can you use the sheet to describe some reasons why each character *es especial*?

Me llamo .... **Me llamo** ....

Tengo .... **años.** **Tengo** .... **años.**

Estoy .... **Estoy** ....

Soy .... **Soy** ....

Me gusta .... **Me gusta** ....

Me gusta .... **Me gusta** ....

Word Bank

		mal	grande	pequeño
amarillo	saltar	María	bien	azul
cuatro	especial	cantar	diez	Pedro

Notes: The directions ask children to describe Pedro and María. Why is Pedro special? Why is María special? Remember, at the beginning of this program, Pedro was three years old, but he celebrated a birthday, and now he is four years old. Answers on the final four lines describing each character may vary.

Lección 8

Puedo, no puedo

Below each picture, write whether or not you can do the action: *puedo* or *no puedo*. Share what you wrote with someone. What can you both do?

....

....

Lección 8

Sí, ¡se puede!

María and Pedro want to know all about you.

Answer the questions to develop a script to say several things about yourself. When you are finished, present your answers to someone. Use the sheet to describe some reasons why you are *especial*.

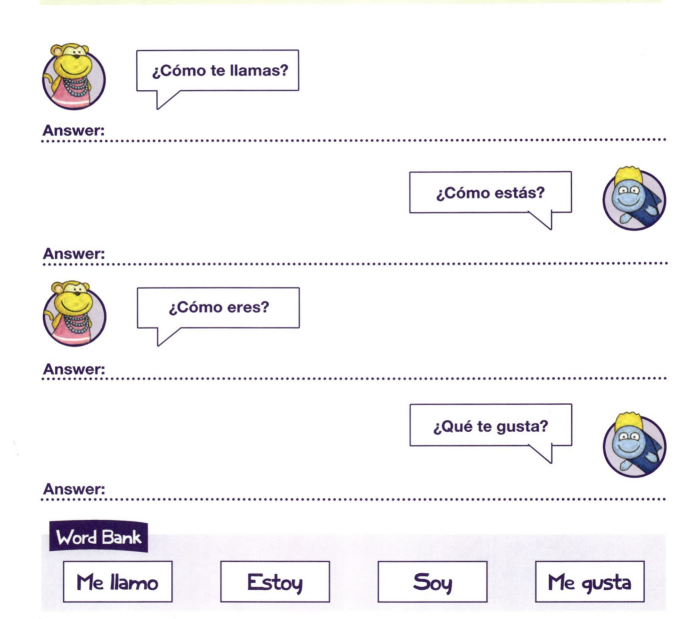

¿Cómo te llamas?

Answer: ....

¿Cómo estás?

Answer: ....

¿Cómo eres?

Answer: ....

¿Qué te gusta?

Answer: ....

Word Bank

| Me llamo | Estoy | Soy | Me gusta |

Note: There aren't many words in the word bank because children should be able to accomplish this activity based on their own vocabulary now. If needed, have children look back at previous activity sheets for help with the questions. Do this activity orally if your children are not ready for writing independently.

The directions ask children to answer Pedro and María's questions to create a dialogue (script). Each child should write answers that describe his or her age, likes, and interests. Answers will vary. After children fill in the blanks, practice asking and answering the questions together.

¿Cómo te llamas?

Hola.
Hola.

Hola.
Hola.

Me llamo Carlos.
Me llamo Carlos.

Y tú, ¿Cómo te llamas?
Y tú, ¿Cómo te llamas?

Me llamo Marta.
Me llamo Marta.

Mucho gusto, Marta.
Igualmente.

Hola a todos

¡Hola a todos! ¡Buenos días,
buenos días, buenos días!
¡Hola a todos! ¡Buenos días,
buenos días, buenos días!

Hola, ¿cómo estás?
¡Yo estoy muy bien!
Vamos a empezar la
clase de español.
Alegres vamos a estar porque
nos gusta mucho cantar.

Hola, ¿cómo estás?
¡Yo estoy muy bien!
Vamos a empezar la
clase de español.
Alegres vamos a estar porque
nos gusta mucho cantar.

¡Hola a todos! ¡Empecemos, empecemos,
empecemos!
¡Hola a todos! ¡Empecemos, empecemos,
empecemos!

Lluvia

Lluvia, lluvia, lluvia, cae, cae así:

Una gota, x-x-x-x

dos gotas, x-x-x-x,

tres gotas, x-x-x-x,

cuatro gotas, x-x-x-x,

cinco gotas, x-x-x-x,

muchas gotas, xxxxxxxx.

¡Seguro me voy a mojar!

¿Cuántos años tienes?

¿Cuántos años tienes?
¿Cuántos años tienes?

Tengo seis años.
Tengo seis años.

¿Cuántos años tienes?
¿Cuántos años tienes?

Tengo doce años.
Tengo doce años.

¿Cuántos años tienes?
¿Cuántos años tienes?

Tengo cuarenta años.
Tengo cuarenta años.

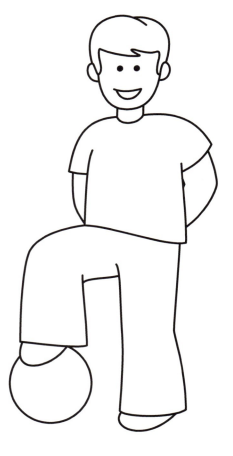

La semana

Lunes,

martes,

miércoles,

jueves,

viernes,

sábado,

domingo.

Elefantes grandes

¡Qué grandes son los árboles!
¡Oh, tan grandes!
Y en los árboles, elefantes saltan.

Derecha, izquierda,
arriba, más arriba.

Saltan, saltan, los elefantes saltan.
¡Elefantes grandes!

Colores, colores

Verde, verde, me gusta el verde.
Verde, verde es el mejor color.
Me gusta el verde, ¿sabes por qué?
Es porque mi papá trabaja en el bosque. (2X)

Rojo, rojo, me gusta el rojo.
Rojo, rojo es el mejor color.
Me gusta el rojo, ¿sabes por qué?
Es porque mi papá es un bombero. (2X)

Blanco, blanco, me gusta el blanco.
Blanco, blanco es el mejor color.
Me gusta el blanco, ¿sabes por qué?
Es porque mi papá es un panadero. (2X)

Azul, azul, me gusta el azul.
Azul, azul es el mejor color.
Me gusta el azul, ¿sabes por qué?
Es porque mi papá es un marinero. (2X)

Negro, negro, me gusta el negro.
Negro, negro es el mejor color.
Me gusta el negro, ¿sabes por qué?
Es porque mi papá es un minero. (2X)

Amarillo, me gusta el amarillo.
Amarillo es el mejor color.
Me gusta el amarillo, ¿sabes por qué?
Es porque mi papá es un taxista. (2X)

Anaranjado, me gusta anaranjado.
Anaranjado es el mejor color.
Me gusta el anaranjado, ¿sabes por qué?
Es porque mi papá siembra naranjas. (2X)

Colores, colores me gustan los colores.
Colores, colores todos lindos son.
Me gustan los colores, ¿sabes por qué?
Es porque mi papá es un pintor. (2X)

Vengan ya

¡Vengan ya, vengan ya!
Vamos a cantar.
La, la, la, la, la, la.
¡Vamos a cantar!

¡Vengan ya, vengan ya!
Vamos a saltar,
a saltar, a saltar
¡Vamos a saltar!

¡Vengan ya, vengan ya!
Vamos a escribir,
a escribir, a escribir.
¡Vamos a escribir!

Bailar

Aplaudir

Correr

Leer

Comer

Reir

Dormir

Caballito blanco

Caballito blanco,
llévame de aquí;
llévame hasta el pueblo
dónde yo nací.

Tengo, tengo, tengo,
tú no tienes nada.
Tengo tres ovejas
en una cabaña.

Una me da leche,
otra me da lana,
otra mantequilla,
para la semana.

Chocolate

Uno, dos, tres, cho;
uno, dos, tres, co;
uno, dos, tres, la;
uno, dos, tres, te;

¡Chocolate! ¡Chocolate!
¡A mí me gusta el chocolate!

calendario

lunes	martes	miércoles	jueves	viernes	sábado	domingo

América del Sur

México, América Central, y el Caribe

España

39

Suggested Answers

Lección 1: Es azul
Answers will vary as children choose different blue items to draw. They should label each item: *Es azul*.

Lección 1: Hola y adiós
1. Hola.
2. Buenos días.
3. Adiós.

Lección 1: ¿Cómo te llamas, animal?
1. Me llamo Pedro.
2. Me llamo Pepe.
3. Me llamo María.
4. Me llamo Camilo.
5. Me llamo Goyo.

Lección 2: ¿Cuántos hay?
1. uno
2. dos
3. dos
4. tres
5. tres
6. uno

Lección 2: ¡Es grande!
1. Vases: the right one is *grande*
2. Tables: the left one is *grande*
3. Houses: the left one is *grande*
4. Milk cartons: the right one is *grande*
5. Cakes: the right one is *grande*
6. Fish: the left one is *grande*

Lección 2: "¿Cuántos años tienes?"
1. Tengo tres años.
2. Tengo cuatro años.
3. Tengo cinco años.
4. Tengo dos años.
5. Tengo diez años.

Lección 3: Diciembre en la familia de María
1. martes
2. miércoles
3. jueves
4. viernes
5. sábado
6. domingo

Lección 3: Día de la semana
1. Es jueves.
2. Es lunes.
3. Es viernes.
4. Es domingo.

Lección 4: Es amarillo
Answers will vary as children choose different yellow items to draw. They should label each item "*Es amarillo.*"

Lección 4: ¿Cómo estás?
Estoy mal.
Estoy bien.
Estoy mal.
Estoy bien.

Lección 4: ¿Bien o mal?
Answers will vary.

Lección 5: ¡Es pequeño!
1. Houses: The right one is *pequeña*.
2. Vases: The left one is *pequeño*.
3. Milk cartons: The left one is *pequeño*.
4. Cakes: The right one is *pequeño*.
5. Fish: The right one is *pequeño*.
6. Tables: The left one is *pequeña*.

Lección 5: ¿Quién dice?
1. Soy pequeño.
2. Soy lista.
3. Soy grande.

Lección 5: Así soy
Answers will vary.

As an example, answers could be:
1. Soy grande.
2. Soy listo.
3. Me llamo Joshua.
4. Tengo 7 años.
5. Estoy bien.

Lección 6: ¿Te gusta?
Answers will vary. Students will illustrate by drawing something blue, a visual of 'singing,' a visual of 'jumping,' and something yellow. They will circle *me gusta* if they like the color/activity and circle *no me gusta* if they do not like it.

Lección 6: ¡Me gusta!
Answers will vary. Students will write *me gusta* next to items they like and *no me gusta* next to items they don't like.

Lección 7: Tengo, no tengo
Answers will vary. Students will circle *tengo* if they have the item (if they have hair, shoes, necklaces, and/or a guitar) and *no tengo* if they do not have that item.

Lección 7: ¿Cantar o saltar?
1. saltar
2. cantar
3. cantar
4. saltar
5. saltar

Lección 7: ¡Soy especial!
The final four lines may vary.

María:
Me llamo María.
Tengo 10 años.
Estoy bien.
Soy lista.
Me gusta saltar.
Me gusta el azul.

Pedro:
Me llamo Pedro.
Tengo 3 años.
Estoy bien.
Soy pequeño.
Me gusta cantar.
Me gusta el amarillo.

Lección 8: Puedo, no puedo
Answers will vary. Students will write *puedo* if they can do the activity pictured and *no puedo* if they cannot.

Lección 8: Sí, ¡se puede!
Answers will vary.

As an example, answers could be:
Me llamo Taylor.
Estoy bien.
Soy grande.
Me gusta cantar.
Me gusta el azul.